MASTER-WORKS

ALBERT W. KETÈLBEY

ALBUM OF FIVE COMPOSITIONS
   (including WEDGWOOD BLUE) ... ...
ALGERIAN SCENE... ... ...
ANGELO D'AMORE ... ...
AN OLD WORLD ROMANCE ... ...
BIRTHDAY GREETING ... ...
BOW BELLS ... ...
BY THE BLUE HAWAIIAN WATERS ... ...
CAPRICE PIANISTIQUE (Piano Novelty)... ... ...
CHAL ROMANO (Overture) ... ...
CHRISTMAS MEDLEY ... ...
CLOCK AND THE DRESDEN FIGURES ...
COCKNEY SUITE ... ...
DANCE OF THE MERRY MASCOTS ... ...
DREAM IDYLL ... ...
DREAM OF CHRISTMAS... ... ...
ELEPHANT'S PARADE ... ...
FAIRIES OF THE STREAM ... ...
FLOWERS ALL THE WAY (Potpourri) ... ...
FROM A JAPANESE SCREEN ... ...
GALLANTRY ... ...
HAPPY RETURNS (Valse Lente) ... ...
HEROES ALL (Quick March) ... ...
IN A CAMP OF THE ANCIENT BRITONS ... ...
IN A CHINESE TEMPLE GARDEN ... ...
IN A FAIRY REALM (Suite) ... ...
IN A PERSIAN MARKET ... ...
IN A PERSIAN MARKET (Easy) ... ...
IN HOLIDAY MOOD (Suite) ... ...

IN THE MOONLIGHT ... ...
IN THE MYSTIC LAND OF EGYPT ... ...
ITALIAN TWILIGHT ... ...
JAPANESE CARNIVAL ... ...
JUNGLE DRUMS ... ...
KNIGHTS OF THE KING (Grand March) ...
LOVE AND THE DANCER ... ...
LOVE'S AWAKENING ... ...
MAYFAIR CINDERELLA ... ...
MY LADY BROCADE ... ...
PICTURES IN MELODY (Selection) ... ...
RECREATION MOMENTS ... ...
REMEMBRANCE (Elegy) ... ...
ROYAL CAVALCADE (March) ... ...
SACRED HOUR ... ...
SANCTUARY OF THE HEART ... ...
SANCTUARY OF THE HEART (Easy) ...
SOUVENIR DE TENDRESSE ... ...
STATE PROCESSION ... ...
SUITE ROMANTIQUE ... ...
SUNBEAMS AND BUTTERFLIES ...
SWEET LOUISIANA (Waltz) ... ...
THREE FANCIFUL ETCHINGS (Suite) ... ...
VALSE APPASSIONATA ... ...
WANDERER'S RETURN ... ...
WEDGWOOD BLUE ... ...
WITH HONOUR CROWNED (March) ...
WITH THE ROUMANIAN GYPSIES ... ...

For Lists of other Arrangements by KETÈLBEY *apply to :—*

BOSWORTH & CO. LTD.

Made in England   Imprimè en Angleterre

IN A PERSIAN MARKET.

Intermezzo-Scene.

ALBERT W. KETÈLBEY.

Synopsis.

The camel-drivers gradually approach the market; the cries of beggars for "Back-sheesh" are heard amid the bustle. The beautiful princess enters carried by her servants, (she is represented by a languorous theme, given at first to clarinet and cello, then repeated by full orchestra)—she stays to watch the jugglers and snake-charmer. The Caliph now passes through the market and interrupts the entertainment, the beggars are heard again, the princess prepares to depart and the caravan resumes its journey; the themes of the princess and the camel-drivers are heard faintly in the distance and the market-place becomes deserted.

"The camel-drivers gradually approach."

"The beggars in the market-place."

(Sing) Back - sheesh, back - sheesh, Al - - - lah,

8ves ad lib.

☆ Back-sheesh = money.   B. & Co. Ltd. 16240

3

4

Back - sheesh, back - sheesh, Al - - - lah, Back - sheesh,

back - sheesh, Al - - - lah, ☆ Emp - shi! emp - shi!

emp - - shi!

fff

sf

☆ Empshi = get away.   B. & C⁰ Ltd. 16240.

"The beautiful Princess approaches."
Poco meno mosso.

"The jugglers in the market-place."

"The snake-charmer."

(Trumpets)

"The Caliph passes through the market-place."

"The beggars are heard again."
(sing) Back-sheesh, back-sheesh, Al - - lah, Back-sheesh, back-sheesh, Al - - lah,

Back-sheesh, back-sheesh, Al - - lah, Emp-shi emp-shi emp - shi!

"The Princess prepares to depart."

"The caravan resumes its journey."

"The market-place becomes deserted."

Printed and bound in Great Britain by
Caligraving Limited Thetford Norfolk

B. & C⁰. Ltd. 16240

7/08(166289)

ALBERT W. KETÈLBEY
ALBUM

OF POPULAR PIECES
for Pianoforte

CONTENTS

BOSWORTH & CO., LTD.
14/15 BERNERS STREET, LONDON W1T 3LJ

Wedgwood Blue
Bleu de Wedgwood   Blaues Porzellan
Intermezzo

Moderato grazioso ♩ = 108   Albert W. Ketèlbey

Sanctuary of the Heart
Sanctuaire du coeur   Des Herzens Heiligtum
Méditation religieuse

Andante sostenuto ♩ = 72   Albert W. Ketèlbey

Gallantry   Galanterie
Intermezzo - Romanze

Moderato con moto ♩ = 108   Albert W. Ketèlbey

In the Moonlight
Sous la Lune   Mondnachtszauber
Poetic Intermezzo

Andante grazioso (poco rubato) ♩ = 72   Albert W. Ketèlbey

Bosworth

14/15 Berners Street,
London W1T 3LJ

ISBN 1-84449-729-1

9 781844 497294

Order No: BOE003774